30 Love Coupons

(25 Pre-Made And 5 Blanks For You to Create)

This Belongs To:

How to use these coupons:

1. Cut out the love coupon you've selected for the day and take a moment to feel gratitude that you are so loved and appreciated by your bestie that got you these coupons... they wanted to give you 30 special happy memories! :-)
2. Give it to your sibling to "cash it in".
3. Enjoy it!!!

Do that one thing i've asked you to do many times before but you never do!

Cook me a 3 course meal or buy me one, lol.
It doesn't have to be fancy :)

Make me a playlist to reflect songs that remind you of me and good times we've had together

A pampering session
for me at my home
organized by you.

Takeaway of my choice

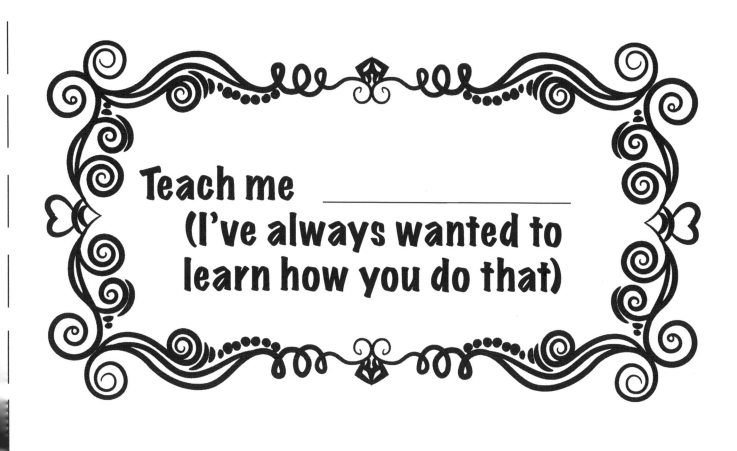

Teach me _____
(I've always wanted to
learn how you do that)

If i've got kids babysit for me
OR
Be my "wing woman/man" for one
night out

Write me a letter or draw me a picture (lol) to express how you feel about our relationship and mail it to me at some point in the next 3 months
(i can't wait to be surprised when i receive it!)

Do a chore of
mine for me

A night where we put our phones away and just hang out without distractions.

I get to keep that thing i "borrowed" from you and have not given back :)

Buy 2 copies of a book you think i'd enjoy reading and lets both read it ... afterwards lets talk about it

I get to pick a thing for us to do together.

A talk session where we can discuss anything i want (and you do your best to share your truth with me even if it's hard or feels weird)

Let's take a weekend trip away to somewhere of my choice.

Cover for me about this one thing

Buy me desert :)

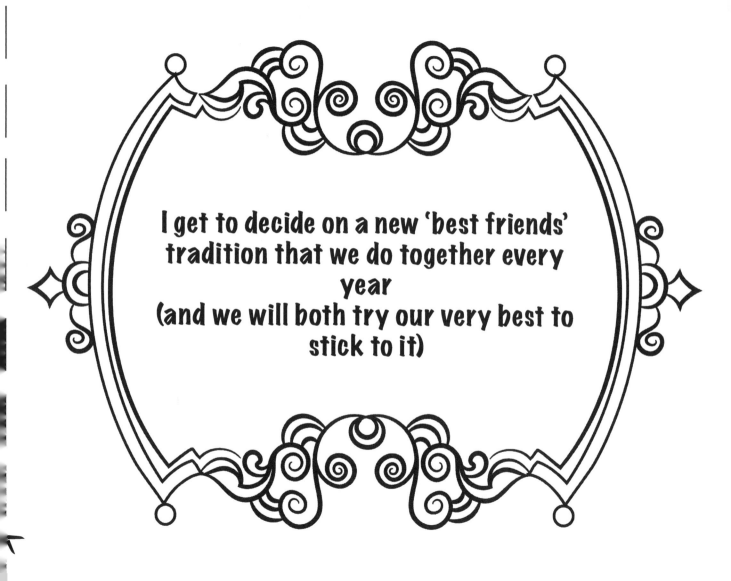

I get to decide on a new 'best friends' tradition that we do together every year
(and we will both try our very best to stick to it)

Made in United States
Orlando, FL
02 April 2024

45371833R00037